T0040485

The Candlelight Master

By the Same Author

POETRY
No Continuing City
An Exploded View
Man Lying on a Wall
The Echo Gate
Poems 1963–1983
Gorse Fires
The Ghost Orchid
Selected Poems
The Weather in Japan
Snow Water
Collected Poems
A Hundred Doors
The Stairwell
Angel Hill

PROSE
Tuppenny Stung: Autobiographical Chapters
One Wide Expanse: Three Lectures
Sidelines: Selected Prose, 1962–2015

AS EDITOR
Causeway: The Arts in Ulster
Under the Moon, Over the Stars: Children's Poetry
Further Reminiscences: Paul Henry
Selected Poems: Louis MacNeice
Poems: W. R. Rodgers
Selected Poems: John Hewitt (with Frank Ormsby)
20th Century Irish Poems
The Essential Brendan Kennelly (with Terence Brown)
Selected Poems: Robert Graves

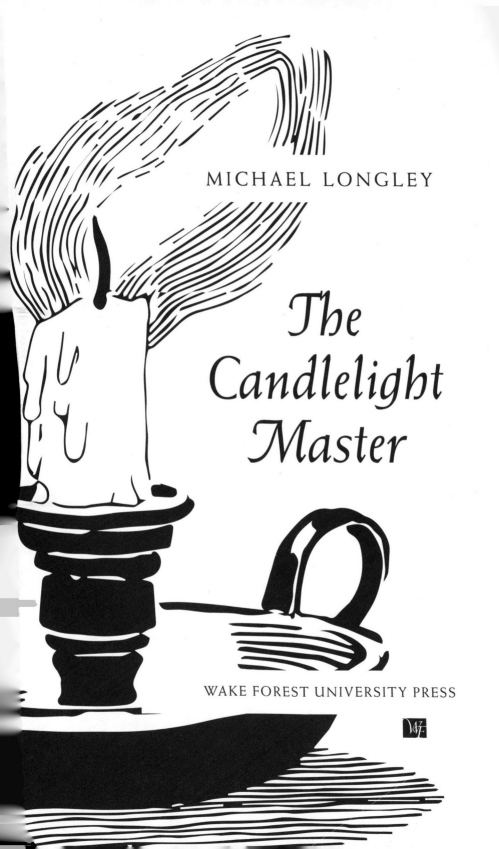

MICHAEL LONGLEY

The
Candlelight
Master

WAKE FOREST UNIVERSITY PRESS

First North American edition

© Michael Longley, 2020

All rights reserved. No part of this book may be
reproduced in any form without prior permission in
writing from the publishers. For permission, write to:

Wake Forest University Press
Post Office Box 7333
Winston-Salem, NC 27109
WFUPRESS.WFU.EDU
wfupress@wfu.edu

ISBN 978-1-930630-93-2 (paperback)
LCCN 2020933450

Designed and typeset by
Nathan Moehlmann,
Goosepen Studio & Press

Publication of this book
was generously supported
by the Boyle Family Fund.

Printed in Canada

for EDNA, *again*

Our bedroom window
Frames a hazel tree:

Your breath on my shoulder's
A catkin shiver.

Contents

And what looks like a zig-zag is really a straight line.

— JOAN MIRÓ

MATISSE

Wielding a colossal pair of scissors,
Cutting out from the costliest paper
The world's peculiar shapes, he instructed
From his wheelchair beautiful assistants
Where to position—floor to ceiling—
Each adhesive genesis, cloud formations
Reflected in estuarial waters.

He covered a stain on his studio wall
With a swallow's cut-out shape, then added
Other birds and fish and coral and leaves,
Memory replacing the outside world
And his imagination a lagoon
Where, immobile, he swam every day
Contemplating his submarine kingdom.

BONNARD

I

Bonnard, bedridden and anxious
That 'the green on the patch of ground
To the left is wrong', arranged
For his nephew Charles to add
To *The Almond Tree in Flower*'s
Blue and white a little yellow,
His last painting of winter's end.
It snowed when he died not long
After the annihilating war,
Each snowflake an alteration.

II

'I should like to arrive
In front of the young painters
Of the year two thousand
With the wings of a butterfly,'
The modest artist said.
On that white table cloth
An Orange-tip alighted.
'I have been trying all
My life to understand
The secret of white.'

ORPEN

Orpen in the trenches
Sketching skeletons—
Breast bone, ankle bone,
Vertebrae, pelvis—
Sets up his easel
On the bomb crater's rim
And paints the armistice.

LEDWIDGE

I can imagine his last sup of tea,
Milky and sweet, elbow on knee, body
Parts, his fingers caressing the mess-tin,
His steamy moustache whispering a girl's name.

GLOSSARY

I meet my father in the glossary
Who carried me on his shoulders, a leg
Over each, hockerty-cockerty, who
Would spend ages poking the kitchen fire,
An old soldier remembering the trenches
And telling me what he saw in the embers,
Battlefields, bomb craters, firelight visions:
A widden-dremer, yes, that's my father.

hockerty-cockerty, seated with one's legs astride another's
shoulders; *widden-dremer*, one who sees visions in the firelight

ORS

I

I am standing on the canal bank at Ors
Willing Wilfred Owen to make it across
To the other side where his parents wait.
He and his men are constructing pontoons.
The German sniper doesn't know his poetry.

II

My daughter Rebecca lives in twenty-four
Saint Bernard's Crescent opposite the home
Wilfred visited for 'perfect little dinners'
And 'extraordinary fellowship in all the arts'.
I can hear him on his way to the Steinthals.

III

Last year I read my own poems at Craiglockhart
And eavesdropped on Robert, Siegfried, Wilfred
Whispering about poetry down the corridors.
If Wilfred can concentrate a little longer,
He might just make it to the other bank.

MAISIE'S POEM

My granddaughter Maisie has written a poem
About the Great War, about 'poppies growing
In the field, growing over the blood'. At seven
She refers obscurely to 'the death of the war'
And then quite clearly to 'raindrops falling
On my face, washing off some of the blood'.

FLOWER-NAMES

for George Larmour

There were twenty-one flavours of ice-cream in the shop
And, in my elegy, twenty-one flower-names: so wrote
Rosetta Larmour, the ice-cream man's mother. Oh,
How I wanted that catalogue to go on forever,
A prayer, a litany of remembered Burren flowers.
The ice-cream man's murder desecrated nature,
Overshadowing crowsfoot, thyme, bog pimpernel
And all our lives and all such coincidences
As Rosetta Larmour's flavours and flower-names.

WAR

I

Because he was his youngest
And dearest child, old Priam
Begged Polydorus not to fight,
But this champion athlete
Wanted to show off his speed
And in a foolhardy display
Raced against the front-runners—
Until he died, for Achilles
Was just as fast and struck him
With his javelin full in the back
Where the golden belt-buckles
Fastened his leather corselet,
The spear-point penetrating
Right through to his navel
And he fell to his knees groaning
And blacking out and clasping
In his hands his intestines.

II

When Hector saw his brother
Polydorus on the ground
Mortally wounded, blacking out,
His intestines in his hands—
His eyes misted over with tears
And he made straight for Achilles
Flaunting his javelin like a flame.

GLORY

Just as through the gorges of a parched mountain-side
All-consuming fire rages and incinerates
Deep forest, blustery winds whirling flames about,
So with his spear Achilles like a god rampaged
Crushing his victims, and the black earth ran with blood;
And just as a farmer yokes broad-browed bulls to thresh
White barley on his well-appointed threshing-floor
And the loud-bellowing bulls quickly husk the grain
Beneath their feet, so beneath almighty Achilles
The heavy-hoofed horses trampled corpses and shields
And blood-gouts churned up by horses' hooves and wheels
Splattered the axle-tree and the chariot-rail, but
The son of Peleus ploughed on in his glory-quest,
His indomitable hands bespattered with gore.

XANTHOS

From under the yoke the shimmering-
Footed chestnut bowed his head, his mane
Streaming from the yoke-pad to the ground,
And answered critical Achilles:

'Balios and I will bring you back safely
This time, fast as a gale-force west wind,
But you yourself are going to die soon
Killed by a god and a mortal man.'

The Furies silenced the talking horse
(Was white-armed Hera a ventriloquist?)
And indignantly Achilles replied:

'I know I am doomed to die at Troy
Far away from my father and mother.
I prepare to die and annihilate.'

EMPTY CHARIOTS

Many horses with high-arching necks
Made their empty chariots clatter along
Down the lines of battle, in mourning
For their irreplaceable charioteers
Who lay on the battlefield, far dearer
To the vultures than to their wives.

BALLYBOLEY

after A. T. Q. Stewart: a found poem

From the window of his cottage
On the edge of the demesne, Lord
Masserine's agent, Samuel Skelton,
Watched the Yeomanry burying-parties
Digging in the hot sun. The bodies
Were shot in, a cartload at a time.
'Where the devil did these rascals come from?'
The officer asked the driver of one cart.
A poor wretch raised a blood-stained face
From the cart and feebly answered:
'I come frae Ballyboley.'
He was buried along with the rest.

MOTHS & BUTTERFLIES

I want to talk to dead children
About moths and butterflies,
The Peacock's eyespots, two
Then four, beauty and terror;
Six Spot Burnet's warning
Black and red (hydrogen
Cyanide); the female
Winter moth that cannot fly;
And one with no proboscis
That cannot feed, a ghetto moth;
Caterpillars that gobble
Stinging nettles and ragwort;
Nightmares of the chrysalis.

In September forty-four
Hanuš Hachenburg writes
Somewhere, far away out there,
Childhood sweetly sleeps
Along that path among the trees;
Listen to Pavel Friedmann
I never saw another
Butterfly, that butterfly
Was the last one, butterflies
Don't live in the ghetto;
I want to talk to dead children,
The children of Terezín,
About moths and butterflies.

DANDELIONS

The children can still be heard,
Their memories growing fainter
And fainter. Listen. Listen.
Just look up to heaven
And think about the violets
One whispers, and another
The dandelions call to me
And the white chestnut branches.

RAVENSBRÜCK

At daily roll-call women prisoners
Stand naked out in the cold for hours.
The guard with a silver-handled whip
Enjoys thrashing, another likes to stamp
In her shiny boots on women's faces.

What do they hear through chattering teeth?
Oh, the prisoners are crying out in pain
And in condemnation of their torturers.
It is Christmas Eve in Ravensbrück. Soon
They will tie together the Virgin's legs.

PRIMO'S QUESTION

How can you murder millions of people
In the middle of Europe and not know?
Look out the window at those miserable lines,
Prisoners fainting and dying of exhaustion
In the long streets and at railway stations.
How can you murder millions and not know?

ECHO

People are like shadows to me
And I am like a shadow

ST CROSS

in memory of Robert Hutchison

Robert is looking through the bird beak window.
The window frame consists entirely of bird beaks.
The space should be full of birdsong but it isn't.
A flock of little birds has been carved out of stone.

THIMBLES

in memory of Catriona Ferguson

I remember her sad humorous eyes
And her collection of thimbles in rows
Hung on the wall beside the fireplace
As though to protect for years to come
Her fingertips from the prick of death.

COUPLETS FOR CLAUDE FIELD

I

You have made a beautiful landscape of old age.
We visit you there, Claude, as on a pilgrimage.

II

You filled the feeders with bird-seed before you died.
You seem to be there, welcoming the passerines.

SEDGE-WARBLERS

Callimachus joins me at your grave
Who shed tears for Heraclitus
And said his poems were nightingales
That death would never lay hands on.
There are no nightingales in Ireland
But sedge-warblers sometimes sing at night
And are mistaken for nightingales,
So death that snatches at everything
Will leave untouched in Bellaghy
Your poems, the sedge-warbler's song.

AFTER AMERGIN

I am the trout that vanishes
Between the stepping stones.
I am the elver that lingers
Under the little bridge.
I am the leveret that breakfasts
Close to the fuchsia hedge.
I am the stoat that dances
Around the erratic boulder.
I am the skein of sheep's wool
Wind and barbed wire tangle.
I am the mud and spittle
That make the swallows' nest.
I am the stonechat's music
Of pebble striking pebble.
I am the overhead raven
With his eye on the lamb's eye.
I am the night-flying whimbrel
That whistles down the chimney.
I am the pipistrelle bat
At home among constellations.
I am the raindrop enclosing
Fairy flax or brookweed.
I am waterlily blossom
And autumn lady's tresses.
I am the thunderstorm
That penetrates the keyhole.
I am the sooty hailstone
Melting by the fireside.
I am the otter's holt and
The badger's sett in the dunes.

I am the badger drowning
At spring tide among flotsam.
I am the otter dying
On top of the burial mound.

PRINTS

Between sand dunes and sea
Under a cloudless sky
A dozen otter prints
Going nowhere it seems,
Mweelrea in the distance
White after last night's fall:
Where will the otter go
Out of the blue this day
Over the sand and snow?

NIGHT

Alcman who kept me awake
In my Trinity rooms
In sixty-two with 'Night'
(*The tops of mountains*
Are asleep, ravines,
Headlands, waterfalls,
The creeping species
That the soil maintains,
Hillside animals)
Follows me to Killary
And Mweelrea across decades
And millennia, from youth
To age, from insomnia
To this lullaby:
(*Long-winged families*
Of birds—all asleep).

A GRASSHOPPER

for Rebecca

On your fiftieth birthday
A memory of you at four
Clambering to a grasshopper's
Song within a drystone wall
And pulling a boulder down
Onto your innocent foot:
After forty-six years accept
As belated medicament
This translation from the Greek
(Anacreon?) which I wrote
When I was less than half your age:

To you, grasshopper, our blessing
When you drink a tiny sip
Of dew and on the petal's tip
Sing your praises like a king:
For all those things are your domain—
All that in the fields you notice,
All that the forest nourishes.
And you are honoured among men,
Sweet prophet of the spring's advance.
The Muses take delight in you,
And Phoebus Apollo too
Who gave you piercing descants.
Age can't reduce you to a ghost,
Wise, earth-born music-lover:
Your body's bloodless and you suffer
Nothing—same as the gods, almost.

Your bandaged foot got better
And the dark bruise disappeared.
I am running out of rhymes,
O fifty-year old daughter,
And I am running out of time.

HELIODORA

Move Meleager to Carrigskeewaun,
Laughing lilies among yellow flags,
Soft narcissus and ragged robin side
By side, myrtle and bog asphodel
(Where does grass of parnassus belong?)
Innocent crocus, dark hyacinth, rose
Weighed down with affection, white violet,
Bright petals for Heliodora's hair,
Her parting immaculate in the breeze,
Who is unlocking the galvanised gate
Or balancing on the Dooaghtry stile
Or shadowing sand dunes at Dadreen,
Heliodora, neither here nor there,
Name-twiner, flower-arranger, dream girl.

ET

It was you who alerted me to *et*
In the love elegies of Propertius,
How it dominates and insinuates,
Separates and joins—an ambiguous word
Et stood for poetry and you and me
Translating from the erotic Latin
'Cupid' and a girlfriend shipwrecked—and death
When my father died and your father died
And we followed Sextus to the black house
And through 'Cornelia', his great death-ode
('May I reach heaven and my ancestors,
My bones conveyed there in the ship of death')
And we took him with us when we married
Enacting that mysterious syllable.

NEW POEM

I dreamed I had discovered a poem by Catullus,
Its shape projected against my eyelids, its pulse
In my ear, its meaning beginning to emerge.
When I woke I translated it into silence.

IN MY SLEEP

I am relieved
You were awake
To hear me speak:
Goodness. Spindrift.

POEM

I am the candlelight master
Striking a match in the shadows.
A smoky wick, then radiance.
I am the candlelight master.

PIETÀ

for Lisa

How compassionate you appear
Bending over your three-year-old
And slipping your little finger
Beneath his penis to lift
The pee-arc away from his clothes.
Did Mary do this for Jesus
Among wood shavings and sawdust?
How tenderly she must have touched.

BIRTH

The cosmos-shaper has come down to earth:
Mary is counting his fingers and toes.

TOES

'Which of my toes is your favourite?'
Amelia asks. Let me nominate
The one gossamer entangles
Or the one cooled by sycamore wings
Or the one sea asters decorate
Or autumn lady's tresses or
The one warmed by a breast feather.
'Which of my feet is your favourite?'
The one stepping over a skylark's
Or a ringed-plover's nest, I'd say.

PRIMARY SCHOOL

I can remember singing at Malone Primary
'Each with his bonny lawss a-dawncing on the grawss'
For the School Inspector; and, late again because
The papers he delivered were late, John McCluskey
Holding out his hand for caning, stumbling to his desk
And swigging consolation from a sludgy inkwell
(Peter my twin and me relishing his grimace);
And Tommy Price peeing high into the girls' toilet
And girls giggling on the other side: 'Is it raining?'
And the second set of twins (from Lancashire) Derek
And Geoffrey, snattery cigarette-card dealers;
And, briefly amongst us, Niall a Dublin boy in whom
Our teacher Mr Maitland suspected treason;
And when the minister came to talk about God,
Our first question: 'Why do Catholics cross themselves?'
And Muriel Bloomfield slipping me a love note,
Stickwoman bride and stickman groom inside a heart;
And Norma Gamble's downy armpits; and Herbie
And Dave grabbing at each other's peckers; and June
Soon to die from a terrible headache; and Mina
And Helen walking behind her coffin; and Alan
Taylor dabbing away tears with a clean hankie.

COURTING COUPLES

We used to spy on the courting couples,
Robin and Jim and I. Barnett's Demesne.
Hillside trees to hide behind. On the slope
Down to the Lagan courting couples lay
And kissed and fondled as it grew darker.

Once, we compared our hairless peckers, Jim
And Robin and I, who are grandfathers now,
And left the courting couples under the trees
Who later would stroll slowly hand in hand
After us into their eighties and nineties.

KEY-CHANGES

in memory of Pamela Rogers

When I was walking past Pamela's house
And she was sitting at her baby grand,
I would pause and let that intimacy
Glimmer through winter-flowering jasmine
Across the little garden towards me
And music-memories out in the cold.

During the moments of my eavesdropping
My twin and I wind up the gramophone,
Five-year-olds, again and again embarking
On that first surge—Tchaikovsky Number One—
A single seventy-eight, fluffy needle,
Opening chords reiterated, loose ends.

Peter and I would fall asleep as Wendy
In the room below practised the Preludes
And Nocturnes, beauty and difficulty, cross-
Hands, her mistakes corrected as we dozed,
A soul-landscape unfolding before us
Thanks to Chopin, Schubert and our sister.

'Last Spring' coincided with puberty:
When I was polishing my Hercules bike
My mother called me inside to listen
On the bakelite wireless in our kitchen
To Grieg's Piano Concerto, and there followed
Liszt, Rachmaninoff, Beethoven, Brahms,

And the rest of Tchaikovsky Number One,
The first movement completed, the second
And third, a concerto like a country,
Hill-tops and lakes, the sea, nowhere to go
But across the border to Finland, bird-
Calls, swans circling overhead, winter angels.

The City of Belfast Symphony Orchestra
In the Ulster Hall, Maurice Miles conducting,
Wrapping me in a swoon of key-changes,
Crescendos and mountainous melodies,
Sibelius Two, later my first LP
Which I would play to exhausted girlfriends.

Courtship was sharing music in the dark,
The sexiness of string quartets—then Fats
And Billie whom I found in Solly's shop
Joined the party: they linger with me now
Outside Pamela's musical household
As she sits down to play her baby grand.

HOCHMAGANDY

after Catullus

I

Be a hinnie, Ispithilla—sorry—
Ipsithilla—inveet me roond tae yer place
Tae join in yer postprandial snoozle—
Lave the door ajee for me—naebody else—
An dinna be stravaigin aff on yer ain
But bide at hame an organise fir us
A wheen o hochmagandy—please, please
Gie me the nod—an emergency call—
Here's me flat on ma back digeestin lunch
Wi ma prick pokin oot o ma toga.

II

At the baths the clivverest claes-sneckers
Are Vibennius an his poofter sin
(Nae fingers mair glutherie than the da's,
Nae hurdies mair hungersome than the sin's).
Why dinna the twasome jist bugger aff
To the erse-hole o naewey—we all knaw
Aboot the da's theftdom, an as fir the sin,
His birsie bum is nae wirth a bawbee.

hochmagandy, fornication; *hinnie*, honey, darling; *ajee*, ajar; *stravaig*, wander; *wheen*, a lot; *claes*, clothes; *sneck*, steal; *sin*, son; *glutherie*, soiled; *hurdies*, buttocks; *hungersome*, hungry; *twasome*, twosome; *naewey*, nowhere; *theftdom*, thieving; *birsie*, hairy; *bawbee*, halfpenny

III

Ye cunt-struck customers o thon bordel
Nine lamp-posts doon frae Saint Whosit's kirk,
D'ye think ye're the only lads wi stanes
An whangs an leeschence for hochmagandy,
An that the lave o us stew like billygoats?
Or because a hundred o ye titlins cram
Up ticht thegither, d'ye think I widnae
Erse-fuck the lot o yiz whaur ye're sittin?
Think whit ye like: fir I'm gaun to scrawl
Filth about yiz all on the knocking-shop-front.
Fir ma lass who has flitted frae ma airms,
On whose bonnie behalf I'm forfochten
(Nae doxy will aye be sae doted on agen)
Is squattin there. Ye're all her lovies noo,
All ye weel-gaithert cockapenties an—worse—
Ye shilpit pervs an poxy kerbcrawlers
An—worst o all—ye, Egnatius, ye,
Prince o the prinkie dudes wi dabberlacks,
Sin o rabbity Spain, yer kenspeckles
Bushy baird an teeth brushed wi Spanish piss.

stane, testicle; *whang*, penis; *leeschence*, license; *lave*, rest, remainder; *stew*,
stink, cause a stench; *titlin*, runt; *forfochten*, exhausted with fighting;
doxy, sweetheart; *weel-gaithert*, rich; *cockapentie*, snob; *shilpit*, puny;
prinkie, foppish, conceited; *dabberlacks*, long lank hair; *kenspeckle*,
distinguishing feature

ANOTHER PIPISTRELLE

Under the arch where house martins nested
I picked up the pipistrelle's skeleton,
A brittle contraption, bones folded
Across the spindly ribcage, the cranium
That had taken in Cardoso's rooftops.

You were affectionate towards my gift
And tore up tissue paper for a shroud
And made your trinket box an ossuary
For a bat that had fallen out of darkness,
Soon to be crossing the Alps to Ireland.

CARDOSO

I

From above the hilltop village
You bring down into the *casa*
A wilting star-of-bethlehem
And keep it alive in tap water
Until the petals close indoors
Showing their melancholy grey-
Green undersides, their afternoon,
Chestnut beams instead of clouds
In this Garfagnana kitchen.

II

Last year with my walking stick
I yanked to the kitchen window
Apricots that tempted neighbours:
A few weeks earlier this year
The apricots are still green
And my only harvest a brown-
Capped blackcap, a female,
A ravenous passerine
Ripening among the branches.

III

Orchid-hunting at Cardoso,
After many early purples
We discover bridal white,
A sword-leaved helleborine
(In Ireland one of the rarest,
One of the most beautiful)
Surviving deer and wild boar
To bring together in its glade
The Garfagnana and Mayo.

HEIFERS

Daphne, dear sister-in-law and farmer's—
Dairy farmer's—wife, at Woodtown Abbott
Make room for Homer who describes how calves—
Heifers to be precise—frisk from their pens
And cavort mooing around their mothers
When the cows return full up from grazing—
He understands that cow-pat atmosphere,
The nursery pens and the milking parlour—
He can make out the milk tanker's rumble
Along the narrow lane to your farmstead.

VICTOR

When Achilles stabs him in the back with a spear-thrust
And Hippodamus gulps out his life bawling like a bull
Dragged by young men to the altar—that takes me back
To the prize bull on the Tyrrells' Kildalkey farm—

Victor—who shuffled across his shitty enclosure
Next to the nursery pens, his mad eye and nose-ring,
His mountainous shoulders and his clammy pizzle,
His elongated dangling scrotum, his bellow.

TO OTOMO YAKAMOCHI

on receiving the inaugural Yakamochi Medal

You, Otomo Yakamochi,
Poet and governor, and I
Minor bureaucrat, and poet too,
Meet across thirteen hundred years
To talk about birds and flowers.

Lover of cuckoos and wisteria,
For you I have saved meadowsweet
And willowherb and loosestrife
And the meadow pipit's few notes
And the skylark's aria.

We gaze on our soul-landscapes
More intensely with every year—
Small boats passing Inishbofin,
Small boats on the Nago Sea,
Wokami River crimson-lustrous.

Barnacle geese our messengers
Across space and time, Otomo—
Tormentil closed by the rain
And centaury, tiny boxes
Yellow and pink, Japanese.

Anything however small
May make a poem, a snail, say,
Tucked into the marram grass,
In the distance Tateyama
Or Mweelrea, holy mountains.

I picture you at the White Strand
Galloping through the breakers,
Spring-tide and rain and spray
Kicked up by your horse's hooves
Drenching bridle and stirrups.

A small townland becomes my life,
Carrigskeewaun, grandchildren
Wading in the tidal channel—
Otomo, my soul's a currach
Disappearing behind the waves.

THE ANTHOLOGIST

Otomo Yakamochi,
Earliest anthologist,
Listened to thousands of poems
And listened to cranes calling
Their mating calls back and forth,
To songbirds among blossoms,
And listened to grasshoppers
And frogs in the harvest fields,
And listened as girls chatted
Up to their knees in shallows
Gathering rock-weed to sell,
And all summer long the snow
Remained on Tachi Mountain,
Sure sign of its divinity.

GRASS OF PARNASSUS

High up on Tateyama
(Of Japan's holy mountains
Yakamochi's favourite)
We find by a stony path
A solitary overlooked
Grass of parnassus in flower
And stoop to decipher
Engraved petals, and to share
Across the millennium
With the flower-loving poet
The white gleam we first noticed
Amid eyebright and speedwell
At far-off Carrigskeewaun
Years ago, and still in bud.

INKWELL

She gave him a sprig of cherry blossom
Which he placed in his inkwell: the black
Wrote its message over every petal.

ANOTHER SANDPIPER

I hear the sandpiper from years ago,
Just there, at the end of the dunes, a peep
Where the lost burial mound used to be.

WILD ORCHIDS

In my synapses early purples persevering
As in a muddy tractor track across the *duach*;
Close to the old well and the skylarks' nest, briefly
Marsh helleborines surviving the cattle's hooves,
Then re-emerging at the waterlily lake
Between the drystone wall and otter corridors;
A stone's throw from the Carrigskeewaun cottage
Two introverted frog orchids; in the distance
A hummock covered with autumn lady's tresses,
Ivory spirals that vanish for a decade;
On the higher bank of the Owenadornaun
Above the sandmartins' nesting holes, butterfly
Orchids like ballerinas; at Kilnaboy
Bee orchids under the sheela-na-gig's display;
Dowdy *neotinea maculata* at my feet
Where the turlough below Mullaghmore disappears
Underground; against limestone grey at Black Head
Red helleborines igniting; the lesser twayblade
With its flower spike like a darning needle, tiny
And hidden away beneath a heather stand;
On the Tyrrells' Kildalkey farm, pink pyramids;
Along the path to the waterfall at Cardoso,
Near Elvira's overgrown olive grove, tongue
Orchids folded like napkins; lizard orchids
In the Mugello, shaggy, thigh-high; on Paros
Bee orchids (again) beside the marble pavement,
A blackcap singing (in Greece or Ireland?); just one
Bedraggled fly orchid in a forgotten field,
Its petals cobalt, chestnut-brown, as I recall.

WASP ORCHID

I

Too late for my catalogue
I learn about the wasp orchid,
A variation of course
On the bee orchid, a long
Narrow wasp-shaped lip and
Bereft of furry side-lobes—
Unencountered until here
And now in County Wexford,
The Raven, to be exact.

II

Retiring from the Senate
Yeats said that he was glad
To be out of politics—
'I'd like to spend my old age
As a bee and not as a wasp'—
And so would I, except there
Might be folk who need to fear
The fretful and cantankerous,
The warning black and yellow.

FEN VIOLET

You paint flowers, Sarah, as though they have souls.
We have stood side by side on Mullaghmore,
Clare's holy mountain, the turlough nearby
With its watery comings and goings,
The diminutive flowers we stoop to see
And christen—pink water-speedwell, say,
Or mudwort—rare flowers—and rarest of all—
Submerged for part of the year—pale yellow,
Pale green—blend your watercolours—fen violet.

MOLY

Translating the *Iliad* at Corragaun—
Book Twenty—Achilles' rampage—
I turn to the *Odyssey* for relief
And stroll from my sheepskin armchair
Down the overgrown pebbly path
To search among goose-grass and centaury
And scarlet pimpernel for that milk-
White flower with black root, so difficult
For mortal man to find, occult herb
And antidote for spells—Circe's spells—
Nobody knows exactly what it is
But I shall recognise it if it's here
(Its name among the gods is Moly)
And Inishturk becomes Ithaca.

EILEAN BÀN

I

Was it a kestrel or merlin
Next to the albino blackbird
In the lighthouse keeper's cottage
Where Gavin Maxwell made his home?
Why does it matter which, or why
That blustery New Year's Eve
At a bend in the cliff path two
Out-of-season primroses
Pointed to the otter's grave?

II

Among the memorabilia
And portraits of his lovers
The stuffed albino blackbird
Seemed to supervise the room
And the neighbourly audience
When I recited my poems
Under the sea eagle's wing
And almost within earshot
Of field mouse and otter.

GYRFALCONS

for David Cabot

Now that you are in your eighties
I look up to you again, perched
On a Nordmarken cliff-edge,
A death-drop on one side, a nest
Of gyrfalcon chicks on the other,
Your dangerous antique camera
Capturing footage to die for
Three decades ago in Greenland:
For a millennium, David,
(Carbon-dated droppings tell us)
Gyrfalcons have been nesting there.

SONNET FOR MICHAEL VINEY

I have walked with him along the yellow strand
Beachcombing for words among hieroglyphics,
And up the hill to a big tarn, around Mweelrea
To Derry, the deserted village, through fences
To oak woods draped with lichens at Old Head
Or Brackloon below Croagh Patrick, and watched
The sun rolling down the Reek, a ball of fire.

He has shown me beetle tracks in the sand dunes,
Microscopic snails, one nearly invisible
Flower called petalwort, a peregrine falcon
And the cloud beyond with its inky rim,
Dead-nettle and chickweed, a stream's tattle.
From his 'thorn-edged acre' at Thallabaun
We gaze into the depths of the Milky Way.

THE WALK

for Jeffrey Morgan

If you hadn't come all the way with me
Along Thallabaun strand when I pointed out
Bottlenose dolphins surfacing between
The islands and suggested they might foretell
An otter if we could brave the sandy wind
And wait for an hour at Allaran Point,
And after only minutes a bitch otter
Paused on rocks just feet away, sea water
Streaming from her whiskers, our thumping hearts
Audible surely, and as we stood to stretch
A family of whooper swans, two white
And three grey, circled above our heads
On their way from Iceland to Carrigskeewaun,
No one would believe these three visitations,
And you quipped what's next then, and yes, old friend,
What's next, what's next, what's next, what's next?

DECEMBER

I shall be eighty soon.
I go on looking for
The Geminids somewhere
Between Cassiopeia
And the big beech tree.

BROTHER

That Catullus line—*multas per gentes*—
Applies to you, my marine engineer
Circumnavigating the globe, and me
Following you in my imagination
Across many a sea to speak in vain
To your ashes. My twin torn from my life,
Accept this elegy wet with my weeping.
Steer your tanker towards eternity—
Greetings, dear sailor, my brother, goodbye.

PETER

My dear twin, seven years a shadow,
Standing beside me on the *duach*,
Sandwort starry at your feet, wild thyme,
Brookweed's minuscule gleam, overhead
The Dooaghtry ravens' conversation
On which we eavesdrop for a moment.

TADPOLES

Amelia spotted tadpoles
In the rainwater puddle
Under the rusting cattle-grid
That marks a boundary between
Thallabaun and Corragaun,
Murky spermatozoa,
A granddaughter's eightieth
Birthday present, she declares,
Our wellies and our shadows
A clattering thunderstorm
In the tadpole universe.

BIRTHDAY PARTY

I turned eighty at Carrigskeewaun
With grandchildren at the table
And in the townland around us
Wheatears and dapper stonechats
And far more lapwings and curlews
Than I expected, a snipe or two,
Ringed-plovers in the middle
Distance on Thallabaun strand
And, where the Owenadornaun
Used to meander, sandpipers
Nervously warming their four eggs.
Wind removed the swallows' nest.
We shall walk hand in hand beyond
Where the burial mound once was.

LOVE

poem beginning with a line of James Schuyler

Give my love to, oh, anybody.
It might as well be Saint Valentine's Day.
I am on my own, if you care to look.
I am standing with my arms stretched wide.

Notes & Acknowledgements

'Ballyboley' versifies a passage from *The Summer Soldiers*, A. T. Q. Stewart's compelling history of the 1798 Rebellion in Counties Antrim and Down.

In 'Moths & Butterflies' and 'Dandelions' I quote from poems in the heartbreaking collection *I Never Saw Another Butterfly: Children's Drawings and Poems from Terezin Concentration Camp, 1942-1944*, edited by Hana Volavkova. 'Moths & Butterflies' was initially commissioned by Carol Ann Duffy for a *Guardian* feature about the alarming decline in insect numbers.

'Primo's Question' was included in *Ghetto*, a chapbook of my poems about the Holocaust (with drawings by Sarah Longley), published in 2019 by Andrew Moorhouse of Fine Press Poetry.

Fourteen of these poems were collected in a pamphlet, *A Stream's Tattle*, Mariscat Press, 2019.

'Echo' is an echo from Gwen John (whose art I revere): a found poem.

'St Cross': the bird beak window can be found at St Cross in Winchester.

'After Amergin' is a refraction of what some consider the earliest poem in Irish, supposedly the work of Amergin, the legendary bard of the Ulster Cycle. The poem was commissioned by Paddy Bushe for the 2018 Amergin Festival in Waterville, County Kerry.

Callimachus, Alcman, Anacreon and Meleager were Greek poets of, respectively, the 3rd, 7th, 6th and 1st Centuries BC.

'Key-changes' was written to commemorate the centenary of the Belfast Music Society. When I worked for the Arts Council of Northern Ireland, Pamela Rogers was the Music Director, a principled colleague and gifted pianist. She was also for a time Chair of the BMS.

'To Otomo Yakamochi': In July 2018 I was honoured to receive the inaugural Yakamochi Medal from the Toyama Prefecture of Japan. Otomo Yakamochi (c. 718–785) was a celebrated poet and politician.

'Wasp Orchid': The poet Mark Roper introduced me to this rare flower. I would not have written my poem without his photographs and telling information.

'Eilean Bàn': I am grateful to Janet Ullman who, in 2018, invited me to give a reading at the Gavin Maxwell house on Eilean Bàn (White Island) near the Skye Bridge.

Acknowledgements are due to the following publications in which some of these poems first appeared: *Agenda, Archipelago, A Bittern Cry, Guardian, Irish Times, London Review of Books, Poetry Ireland Review, Reading the Future, Yellow Nib;* and to the BBC and RTÉ.

A few words might require a gloss: *holt* is an otter's den, and *sett* a badger's den; *townland* is a rural term for an area of land that varies from a few acres to thousands; *duach* in Mayo means a sandy plain behind dunes that affords some pasturage (the same as *machair* in Scots); *yellow flags* are wild irises; the *Geminids* are a meteor-shower that appears in mid-December; in Mayo the local name for Croagh Patrick is the *Reek.*

I thank Sarah Longley for her lovely cover drawing. The distinguished Greek scholar Maureen Alden continues to be an inspiration. The first readers of these poems have been, as always, Edna Longley, Fran Brearton, Frank Ormsby and Patricia Craig. I am very grateful to all four of them.

dust motes make visible
gossamer overhead

lying side by side
remembering passion

we climb gossamer and
dust motes to the ceiling